SLAVE LIFE ON A SOUTHERN PLANTATION

SLAVE LIFE ON A SOUTHERN PLANTATION

ASHLEY NICOLE

MASON CREST
PHILADELPHIA | MIAMI

MASON CREST

450 Parkway Drive, Suite D, Broomall, Pennsylvania 19008
(866) MCP-BOOK (toll-free) • www.masoncrest.com

© 2020 by Mason Crest, an imprint of National Highlights, Inc.

Printed and bound in the United States of America.

CPSIA Compliance Information: Batch #RGSL2019.
For further information, contact Mason Crest at 1-866-MCP-Book.

First printing
1 3 5 7 9 8 6 4 2

ISBN (hardback) 978-1-4222-4406-7
ISBN (series) 978-1-4222-4402-9
ISBN (ebook) 978-1-4222-7421-7

Library of Congress Cataloging-in-Publication Data
on file at the Library of Congress

Interior and cover design: Torque Advertising + Design
Production: Michelle Luke

Publisher's Note: Websites listed in this book were active at the time of publication. The publisher is not responsible for websites that have changed their address or discontinued operation since the date of publication. The publisher reviews and updates the websites each time the book is reprinted.

QR CODES AND LINKS TO THIRD-PARTY CONTENT

You may gain access to certain third-party content ("Third-Party Sites") by scanning and using the QR Codes that appear in this publication (the "QR Codes"). We do not operate or control in any respect any information, products, or services on such Third-Party Sites linked to by us via the QR Codes included in this publication, and we assume no responsibility for any materials you may access using the QR Codes. Your use of the QR Codes may be subject to terms, limitations, or restrictions set forth in the applicable terms of use or otherwise established by the owners of the Third-Party Sites. Our linking to such Third-Party Sites via the QR Codes does not imply an endorsement or sponsorship of such Third-Party Sites or the information, products, or services offered on or through the Third-Party Sites, nor does it imply an endorsement or sponsorship of this publication by the owners of such Third-Party Sites.

TABLE OF CONTENTS

KEY ICONS TO LOOK FOR:

Words to Understand: These words with their easy-to-understand definitions will increase the reader's understanding of the text while building vocabulary skills.

Sidebars: This boxed material within the main text allows readers to build knowledge, gain insights, explore possibilities, and broaden their perspectives by weaving together additional information to provide realistic and holistic perspectives.

Educational videos: Readers can view videos by scanning our QR codes, providing them with additional educational content to supplement the text. Examples include news coverage, moments in history, speeches, iconic sports moments, and much more!

Text-Dependent Questions: These questions send the reader back to the text for more careful attention to the evidence presented there.

Research Projects: Readers are pointed toward areas of further inquiry connected to each chapter. Suggestions are provided for projects that encourage deeper research and analysis.

Series Glossary of Key Terms: This back-of-the-book glossary contains terminology used throughout this series. Words found here increase the reader's ability to read and comprehend higher-level books and articles in this field.

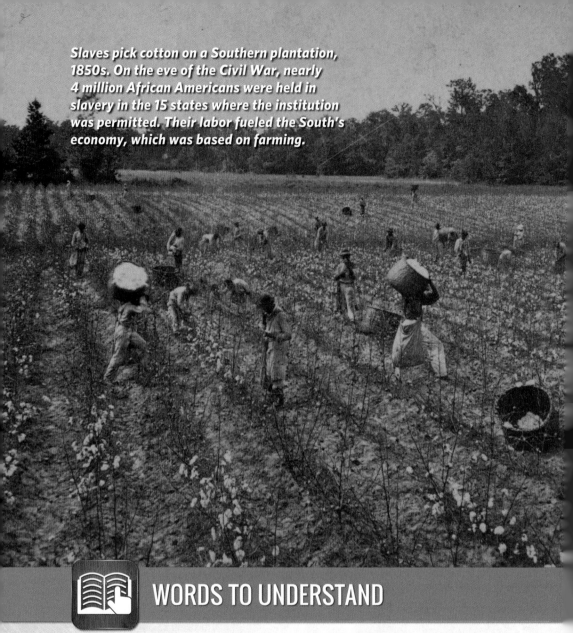

Slaves pick cotton on a Southern plantation, 1850s. On the eve of the Civil War, nearly 4 million African Americans were held in slavery in the 15 states where the institution was permitted. Their labor fueled the South's economy, which was based on farming.

WORDS TO UNDERSTAND

An **abolitionist** was an individual who was fighting for the anti-slavery cause. Many abolitionists were former slaves themselves.

Commodity crops are crops that are easily traded and stored. They are also often grown in large quantities.

The **textile industry** concerns the design, production, and distribution of cloth and clothing. In the antebellum South, the textile industry relied heavily on cotton.

CHAPTER 1

Overview of Plantation Slavery

Frederick Douglass was about twenty years old when he fled successfully to New York City and then Massachusetts, eluding slavery. Five years earlier, his plot to escape with several other slaves had been discovered and foiled. Douglass had changed his last name from Bailey to better hide from those who might be looking for him. The former slave would go on to become one of the most prominent speakers for abolition in the United States, and he had the experience to back him up.

Earlier in his life, Douglass had been separated from his mother, who was also a slave. His father had been a white man whom Douglass never met. For eight years, Douglass lived with his grandmother on a Maryland plantation. At that point, he was sold to a home in Baltimore. There, his mistress taught him how to read in spite of state laws prohibiting such education. When Douglass was sixteen, his master died. The teenage slave was sent back to the fields in Maryland.

It was in 1833 that Douglass made his first attempt to escape slavery, but it would be five more years before he was successful. Soon, Douglass was called to speaking engagements to discuss his anti-slavery stance, establishing himself as a prominent figure in the **abolitionist** movement. By this point, he had endured more than anyone's fair share of pain, but he would prove an enduring force in the fight against slavery in America.

Frederick Douglass escaped from slavery and became an important leader in the abolitionist movement. He was a talented speaker and writer.

A BRIEF HISTORY OF SLAVERY IN THE UNITED STATES

In 1619, a Dutch ship brought twenty slaves from Africa to the settlement of Jamestown, Virginia. The slaves had been captured from a Spanish ship and baptized, so the Europeans opted to use them as indentured servants. Indentured laborers from Britain were a precursor to slavery, but they were only required to work for a few years. Indentured servants would agree to work for a specific amount of time before they were allowed to go free. Essentially, they earned their freedom through hard labor.

Eventually, the laws made it such that people brought over from "non-Christian" African nations could be made slaves indefinitely. In the past, customs and laws had made it such that Europeans did not force into slavery anybody who had been baptized into Christianity. This would change as the popularity of slavery grew in the United States.

Eventually, European settlers found that African slaves were cheaper than indentured servants from Europe. Before slavery, the colonists at Chesapeake Bay had found it difficult to attract and maintain workers due to the harsh conditions of the frontier. The colonists needed to find a way to attract workers to work on their farms, all the while operating with little money to pay laborers. As plantations and farms spread throughout the South, a growing need for cheap labor encouraged the expansion of slavery.

The slave trade was part of a triangle. The Americas would send sugar, tobacco, and cotton to Europe. From Europe, ships would take textiles, rum, and other goods to Africa. Then, ships would bring slaves from Africa back to the Americas.

Congress abolished the transatlantic slave trade (but not slavery) in 1808. In spite of the fact that the slave trade was illegal, domestic trade and illegal overseas trade were still common. For a time, it seemed as if nothing could prevent the demand for slavery, especially in the growing cotton industry of the southern states.

THE ECONOMIC ROOTS OF SLAVERY

In the South, plantation slavery was viewed as a requirement for economic success. In fact, plantation slavery was a major contributing factor to the profitability of crops like cotton and rice. Small farmers could churn a profit, but they were by no means the agricultural powerhouses of the region. Plantations might have around fifty slaves, whereas small farmers might have just a handful. Conditions for slaves on each type of property could differ significantly, as did the conditions of different positions on the property.

In the earliest days of United States history, no laws existed surrounding slavery. In 1640, Virginia courts sentenced an African man, John Punch, to slavery after he tried to run away from his indentured servitude. The white men he'd escaped with were sentenced to only a few extra years of servitude. This set early precedent for black and white servants to be treated differently, though this was surely not the first time that had happened.

The role of indentured servitude and slavery became significant as the South developed an economy based on agriculture and **commodity crops**, which were typically labor-intensive. Plantations prospered by growing tobacco, rice, and indigo in the

This advertisement in a Charleston, South Carolina, newspaper, circa 1780, notes that a group of slaves for sale are from the "Windward & Rice Coasts." This was an area of West Africa where rice was traditionally grown. American colonists had little experience with this crop, so slaves who knew how to plant, harvest, and process rice were very valuable.

earliest days, and after 1790 the South relied heavily on cotton to produce goods.

Initially, most slaves were men. For many plantations, young men were the preferred slaves because they were strong and could perform tasks quickly and efficiently. Soon enough, some slave owners found that women were more affordable and more widely available for their fields. In an additional twist, slave owners would also go on to use only black men as skilled laborers like blacksmiths and carpenters, leaving primarily women and their children to work in the fields.

Slavery was not considered widespread in the northern states and was abolished in many of them by the early 1800s, but this did not mean northern Americans did not benefit from the practice. Slavery made many northern businessmen rich. Additionally, many of the people who were opposed to slavery in the northern states did not necessarily have moral qualms about it. Some thought it was poor business practice.

THE ROLE OF TECHNOLOGY IN SLAVERY

Technology was intrinsic in the development of slavery. One important invention saved time and labor. However, it created a greater demand for slaves, rather than lowerering the need for slave labor, because this invention allowed more tasks to be completed in a shorter time frame.

Until the late eighteenth century, the main problem with processing cotton had been that the seeds were so hard to separate from the cotton itself. Each piece of fiber had to be cleaned by hand, so it would take a laborer an entire day to clean about one pound of cotton. To meet the needs of the growing **textile**

SLAVE REBELLIONS

As a result of some of the working and living conditions, slaves would occasionally rebel. They sometimes poisoned their owners, destroyed machinery, or burned down buildings and farms. Some slaves even harmed themselves so they would be worth less money if a master tried to sell them. Some mothers killed their young infants so that they would not be forced to live in slavery.

In 1800, Gabriel Prosser planned a rebellion in Richmond with a group of other slaves. Prosser, who may not actually have gone by this name, was a blacksmith who had learned how to read. As summer approached, the slaves sought sympathy for their cause. While no white men died in the rebellion, the state executed Gabriel and 26 other rebels.

Generally, large-scale rebellions like Gabriel's were unsuccessful. Nat Turner's 1831 rebellion was the scariest and most threatening to white slaveowners. Turner's group of 75 black slaves killed 60 white people in a matter of two days. The rebellion was stopped by a state militia and local resistance. As a result of the fear white slaveowners felt, they painted an even stronger picture of black slaves as barbarians who required strict control.

industry in Europe and the northeastern states, cotton farmers needed to streamline the process of cleaning cotton so that they could meet the economic demand.

In the 1790s, Eli Whitney developed the cotton gin, a device that could quickly and easily remove seeds from cotton fibers. The hand-cranked cotton gin could clean about fifty pounds of cotton in a single day. This made cotton much more profitable than rice and tobacco. Unlike food crops, cotton was also easy to store for a longer period of time. As a result of the new technology, Southern plantation owners who lived in cotton-growing areas increased the amount of land they devoted to growing cotton.

While one might initially believe that Whitney's cotton gin made the lives of slaves in the South easier, this is not the case. More land for cotton farming required more slaves to tend and

Slaves bring cotton to be processed in a hand-cranked cotton gin, while plantation owners tally the profits.

pick the cotton. As a result, the number of slaves in the cotton-producing areas of the Deep South grew.

THE QUALITY OF LIFE FOR SOUTHERN SLAVES

While slavery became more popular and economical, the truth is that it may have led to worsened conditions for those forced into labor. Misinformation and misunderstanding of those who were not white developed during this time period as well, leading to dangerous and deadly conditions at times.

Slaves suffered tremendously at the hands of their owners, and medical care was scant. As a result, enslaved workers died from a wide variety of conditions, from childbirth complications to infections caused by shackles and other forms of punishment. Medical professionals would often even experiment on slaves, putting them in their own wards or hospitals.

Quality of life also decreased when conditions became more crowded. In addition to poor treatment from slave owners, slaves also had to contend with harsh working conditions, meager nutrition, and emotional distress. For example, mothers and their children could be separated without a moment's notice. As a result, slaves would be forced to hide their children from their owners.

A GROWING PROBLEM

Slaves were beginning to make up a significant portion of the population in some of the bigger cities in the southern states. The growing proportion of slaves was becoming impossible to ignore by the time the Civil War broke out, and the restless nature of slaves who were focused on abolishing the practice was increasingly prominent as well.

Between the 1830s and 1860s, abolitionists took many steps toward abolishing slavery. Frederick Douglass and author Harriet Beecher Stowe both wrote books that established sympathy toward slaves. Douglass gave a speech in which he stated, "No man can put a chain about the ankle of his fellow man without at last finding the other end fastened about his own neck." Abolitionists were heating up the debate regarding slavery. Douglass would even go on to work as an adviser to President Abraham Lincoln.

The 1830s also brought about the popularity of the Underground Railroad, a process through which slaves could escape to the northern states. Harriet Tubman, a former slave, was a major force in helping slaves escape. In a letter from Douglass to Tubman, he wrote, "The midnight sky and the silent stars have been the witnesses of your devotion to freedom and of your heroism. Excepting John Brown—of sacred memory—I know of no one who has willingly encountered more perils and hardships to serve our enslaved people than you have."

Due to numerous compromises between the northern and southern states, slavery would last until the Civil War ended in 1865. That year, the Thirteenth Amendment to the Constitution was ratified, declaring slavery to be illegal in the United States.

Scan here to learn more about Harriet Tubman's life.

TEXT-DEPENDENT QUESTIONS

1. Why did slave owners initially prefer young men as slaves, and why did this change?
2. When did Congress abolish the slave trade?
3. What Constitutional amendment finally abolished slavery?

RESEARCH PROJECT

Choose a former slave, like Frederick Douglass, to research at your school's library or on the Internet. How did this individual enter slavery? Did they ever escape? If so, how? Create a timeline with several major life events from this person's life and share it with your class.

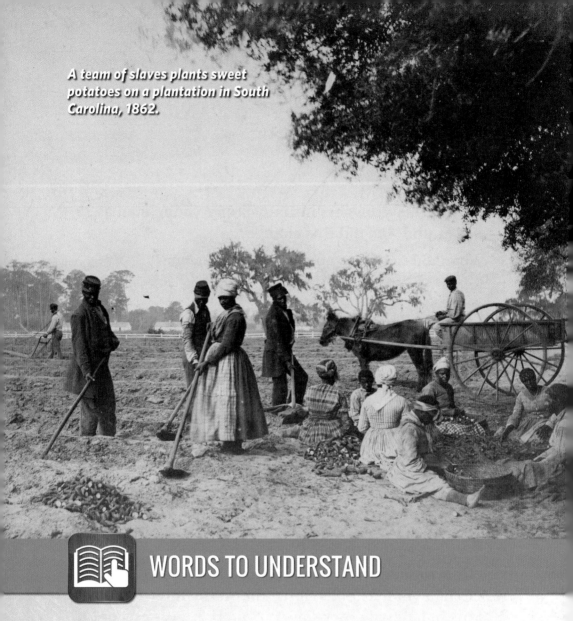

A team of slaves plants sweet potatoes on a plantation in South Carolina, 1862.

Threshing is the act of separating grain from a plant, especially with a flail or other revolving tool. Corn and rice might require threshing.

An **overseer** is an individual, not a slave, tasked with overseeing the slaves. He or she might punish slaves if they don't meet their quotas.

Slaves were treated like **chattel**, which means they were treated like personal possessions or property.

CHAPTER 2

Slave Duties

Not all slaves were treated alike. In fact, slaves who worked in houses and those who worked in fields lived distinct lives. As a result, many differing slave narratives exist. Slaves had difficult experiences no matter where they worked, though the extent of such difficulties varies across the board.

Also of note is the fact that slaves could be selected for their duties based on the color of their skin. Slaves with a darker skin were considered more suitable for work in the fields, but slaves who had lighter skin were deemed suitable for working in a domestic setting. Additionally, sometimes the slaves with lighter skin were actually descendants of the slave owner. As a result, the slave owner might allow these children to work in the home.

No matter where a slave worked, their duties were expansive. Slave life was not easy for anybody, whether they worked in the fields or worked inside the plantation home.

THE DUTIES OF SLAVES WORKING IN FIELDS

For slaves who worked in fields, a typical work day started when the sun rose and ended when the sun went down, perhaps longer than twelve hours a day. According to a slave named Moses Grandy, slaves would work until noon before they could have even a bite of food. Men, women, and children were all treated equally in this manner.

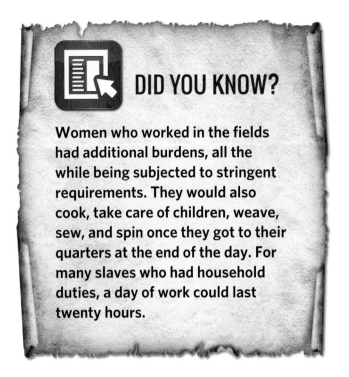

DID YOU KNOW?

Women who worked in the fields had additional burdens, all the while being subjected to stringent requirements. They would also cook, take care of children, weave, sew, and spin once they got to their quarters at the end of the day. For many slaves who had household duties, a day of work could last twenty hours.

Additionally, slaves had limited access to drinking water. He wrote, "Our drink was the water in the ditches, whatever might be its state; if the ditches were dry, water was brought to us by boys. The salt fish made us always thirsty, but no other drink than water was ever allowed. However thirsty a slave may be, he is not allowed to leave his employment for a moment to get water; he can only have it when the hands in working have reached the ditch at the end of the rows."

On plantations, slaves who worked in fields were tasked with clearing land, digging ditches, cutting wood, hauling supplies, slaughtering animals, and repairing buildings. Some slaves were tasked with duties associated with livestock, which could involve feeding them or cleaning up after them.

An escaped slave, William Wells Brown, reported that one plantation required men to pick eighty pounds of cotton each day and women to pick seventy pounds. Anybody who failed to meet this quota would be whipped for each pound he or she was short. Slaves often had to meet the same requirements whether they were weak and frail or young and strong. As a result, slaves were forced to work quickly and without concern for their own well-being. According to Solomon Northrup, the cotton picking season would start in August. Each slave would have a sack to fill, and "A strap is fastened to it, which goes over the neck, holding the mouth of the sack breast high, while the bottom reaches nearly to the ground. Each one is also presented with a large basket that will hold about two barrels."

On large plantations, the slaves were often supervised by an **overseer**. According to Grandy, "the overseer stood with his watch in his hand, to give us just an hour; when he said 'rise,' we had to rise and go to work again." An overseer could at any time opt to beat the slaves any way they saw fit.

Other times, plantations used a driver. A driver was also a slave, which could lead to conflict between slaves and drivers. According to Grandy, "one black man is kept on purpose to whip the others in the field; if he does not flog with sufficient severity, he is flogged himself: he whips severely, to keep the whip from

A white overseer (right) watches a group of slaves toiling on a South Carolina cotton plantation. Overseers were pressured by the plantation owners to get the most work possible out of their slaves, in order to maximize the plantation's profits.

A black male driver (standing, wearing hat) oversees the work of many female slaves on a cotton plantation, 1860s.

his own back." In spite of the fact that they seemingly had power, drivers were constantly under threat.

Some slaves were skilled in agriculture and were held responsible for making important decisions for the plantation. They determined when crops were ready to harvest or how to pack different crops for transport, for example.

THE DIFFERENCES BETWEEN PLANTATION SLAVES AND SMALL FARM OR URBAN SLAVES

Slaves who worked on smaller farms could potentially have better relationships with their owners, but this was not a guarantee. Owners who lived on small farms might have a more personal connection with their slaves because of the fact that they were likely to work together or live in closer quarters. Rather than having fifty slaves, a small farm owner might have just a few.

The size of the farm had a direct connection to the type of crop planted there. Especially early on, expansive plantations tended toward sugar and rice. On the other hand, slaves on smaller farms might cultivate tobacco instead.

Then, there were some slaves who worked in small shops. These slaves often had marketable skills and lived in urban areas. They often worked alongside tailors, butchers, masons, and other skilled workers. This could build tension with skilled white workers, who saw the slaves becoming increasingly useful in these environments.

Other urban slaves would perform tasks in shipyards, brickyards, and warehouses. Ultimately, these urban workers were said to have more favorable lives than their rural counterparts. They had more access to information and social lives in many situations. According to Frederick Douglass, "A city slave is almost a freeman, compared with a slave on

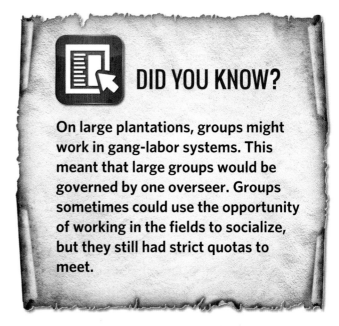

DID YOU KNOW?

On large plantations, groups might work in gang-labor systems. This meant that large groups would be governed by one overseer. Groups sometimes could use the opportunity of working in the fields to socialize, but they still had strict quotas to meet.

This photo, in an ornate frame, shows a slave nursemaid holding a white child. The photo came from a cotton plantation in the Mississippi Delta region of eastern Arkansas.

the plantation. He is much better fed and clothed, and enjoys privileges altogether unknown to the slave on the plantation."

THE DUTIES OF DOMESTIC SLAVES

Slaves who worked inside plantation homes had somewhat better working conditions. They had better access to clothing and food sometimes. Domestic slaves provided much different services, but this does not mean they had easy lives. They were under constant stress and pressure of their masters, and they had very little privacy compared to those who worked in the fields.

The duties of domestic slaves tended toward cooking, cleaning, and serving meals. Some slaves washed laundry, cleaned floors, or took care of the grounds surrounding the home. They might quilt or sew as well.

Many domestic slaves cared for the children of the slave masters. They would be nannies for small children, perhaps even caring for their own children as well. Men who worked in domestic positions might drive their owners around or perform other errands that might take them outside the house.

As a result of spending so much time in the home, women who worked as domestic slaves might develop stronger relationships with their mistresses. In fact, some women even served as midwives for their mistresses who gave birth.

SLAVE WORKING CONDITIONS

The working conditions for slaves were harsh and unforgiving. One component that made this so was the punishment divvied out by drivers, overseers, and slave owners. Lashes were a common punishment for slaves who did not perform the tasks required of them. Lashes and other type of physical abuse were only one incentive used to keep slaves working, and slave owners who saw their slaves as **chattel** did not feel bad about issuing such punishment.

Slave owners also used incentives as a means of motivating slaves to work harder or faster. A slave owner might use food or better working conditions as a means of encouragement. But just as easily as food could be given, it could be taken away.

Scan here to learn more about the rice plantations of the South.

Different fields had different types of working conditions that posed their own challenges. For sugar plantations, slaves would be divided by their levels of strength. The strongest workers would handle planting, spreading manure, and cutting the sugar cane. The weaker workers would handle other tasks. Children and the elderly would handle tasks like scaring away birds and guarding crops. On sugar plantations, every slave was put to work because there were so many steps to fulfill in the process.

Slaves who worked in tobacco fields sometimes worked on smaller plantations with fewer slaves. They would have fewer slaves working around them, and they could often work alongside each other. Tobacco fields were more common throughout the mid-Atlantic region of the United States, and temperatures were less tropical than in Louisiana. Mortality rates for slaves living on tobacco plantations were often lower than the rates for slaves living on sugar plantations.

The conditions in the rice fields were often the worst for slaves because they were forced to stand in water for long periods of time, which could lead to infection. The slaves would often have to clear swampy lands and use their feet to distribute the rice seedlings. The process of **threshing** the fields was also tedious and strenuous, potentially leading to injury.

Working conditions were also dependent upon the weather of the region in which the plantation was situated. For example, sugar plantations might be situated in Louisiana, which offered a humid climate. Those working in these conditions would be more at risk for health conditions like smallpox, dysentery, and typhoid. Mortality rates of slaves in these conditions was quite high.

Slaves were expected to work in all varieties of conditions. Whether they were sick, injured, or pregnant, they would be forced to work or face extreme punishment. The goal of a slave owner was certainly to get the most labor out of slaves, regardless of what they were feeling.

TEXT-DEPENDENT QUESTIONS

1. What types of duties did slaves perform inside the plantation homes?
2. Which type of slave was more likely to perform midwifery duties?
3. What types of duties did urban slaves perform?

RESEARCH PROJECT

Imagine yourself as a slave working in either a plantation home or in the fields. Write a diary entry from the perspective of a slave in this position, discussing your work day. What tasks did you do? Who did you talk to? How did you feel? Write at least two pages.

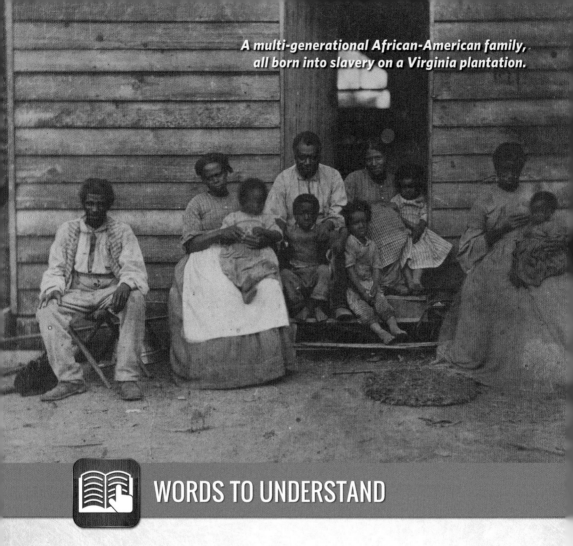

A multi-generational African-American family, all born into slavery on a Virginia plantation.

WORDS TO UNDERSTAND

Somebody who has been **coerced** has been talked into something or feels forced to engage in an activity.

A **communal** society is one that shares resources and responsibilities amongst the community members.

Recuperating is the process of healing or recovering from something, including physical trauma like childbirth.

A **surrogate** is a substitute. For example, a surrogate mother is somebody who carries a fetus to term if the mother is unable to.

A community that is **matrifocal** is focused on motherhood. The mother is the head of the household or family.

CHAPTER 3

Family Life on the Plantation

In spite of how slave owners might have felt, the life of a slave did not end at the end of the work day. Slaves had complex relationships with each other. Family life was much different for non-slaves than for slaves. Slaves had to learn to adapt to family conditions in ways that their white owners would never be able to identify with.

THE MARRIAGES OF SLAVES

Some masters might arrange courtships between their slaves. For example, domestic workers would often pair up with other domestic workers. Slaves who worked in fields might marry each other. This was also practical, considering the fact that slaves who worked in close proximity would be more likely to build relationships.

In many cases, courtship rituals were not unlike those of white people. According to an article in the *Journal of American Folklore*, "The slave girl had to be won as surely as did her fair young mistress, and her black fellow in slavery who aspired to her hand had to prove his worthiness to receive it." Often, an older man would instruct the younger men how to court women.

Often, men did not want to marry women from the plantations in which they lived. One common reason for this was the fact that the husband would have to watch his wife face extreme punishment, potentially on a daily basis. They would be powerless

Scan here to watch a video about the role of families in slavery.

to protect their wives and would instead have to witness every beating without acting. Slaves who worked in town tended to find mates easier than those who worked in rural areas with few neighbors.

Unfortunately, marriage was not considered valid or legal for slaves in most circumstances, so an owner could decide to split up the couple at any moment, perhaps selling them to different owners. Moses Grandy witnessed his own wife being sold from a nearby plantation to a new owner. He never saw her again. A Presbyterian pamphlet from Kentucky published in 1835 said, "For, all the regulations on this subject would limit the master's absolute right of property in the slaves. In his disposal of them he could no longer be at liberty to consult merely his own interest . . . their present quasi-marriages are continually voided (at the master's pleasure)."

Grandy's heartbreaking tale about watching his wife leave is by no means the only one. The Presbyterian pamphlet also describes the slaves and the horror they felt with, "Brothers and sister, parents and children, husbands and wives, are torn asunder and permitted to see each other no more. These acts are daily occurring in the midst of us."

After a male slave was sold, an owner might assign his wife to a new husband. The same might apply if a couple was not having children. The owner might assign each person to a different partner in the hopes it would speed up reproduction. Women who did not have children were at high risk of being sold. Additionally, the death of a slave owner could mean the splitting up of families to different plantations under new owners.

In some cases, a marriage could give slaves the power to negotiate with their masters. For instance, they might present a marriage to their master in the hopes that he or she will opt out of selling one of them so that they can have children. In other cases, an owner wouldn't want to sell one partner out of fear that the other would run off.

GIVING BIRTH AND RAISING CHILDREN AS A SLAVE

Enslaved women who came from Africa had different experiences in the labor and delivery process than their American-born counterparts. The women who were born in America tended to have higher birthrates, and they also tended to have children earlier than their mothers.

In the antebellum South, people did not necessarily give birth in hospitals. In fact, the labor and delivery process for slaves was often not even overseen by a medical doctor. Rather, a midwife or fellow female slave would take on the role of delivering the baby. Those who worked as midwifes might learn the skill from an older female relative.

Pregnancy was difficult for slave women who were forced to continue working, and many women died in childbirth during this time period. For those who did survive, getting back to work quickly was critical. Some plantations might give a **recuperating** slave just a couple days to come back to the fields. If the woman had suffered complications in the process and was no longer able to work as well, her owner might sell her.

As states established laws regarding slavery, Virginia

determined that all children would take the status of "free" or "slave" from their mother. This meant that a white man could assault a slave, and her children would be deemed slaves as well. Other states would follow suit with similar laws.

Just as husbands and wives could be separated by sale during slavery, the same applied to children and parents. Grandy remembers having four sisters and four brothers, but he also claims that his mother had more children. The other children died quite young or were sold to other owners. "My mother often hid us all in the woods, to prevent master selling us," he wrote. This is just one example of the terror a mother could feel watching her child be sold into the cruel and terrible reality of slavery.

If a mother resisted the sale of her children, she could be beaten and tied up as punishment. Some slave owners would use the threat of selling children as a way of keeping women under control. In some cases, mothers would allegedly kill their own newborns so that they could avoid the horrors of slavery as they grew up.

Slave was a drastic change for African women. In Africa, many women primarily served as mothers and caretakers. In the United States, these women were now forced laborers first and mothers

Plantation owners bid on an enslaved woman at an auction in Richmond, Virginia, in 1856.

second. They had little power over their children's well-being, especially because women who gave birth had just multiplied their owner's economic status.

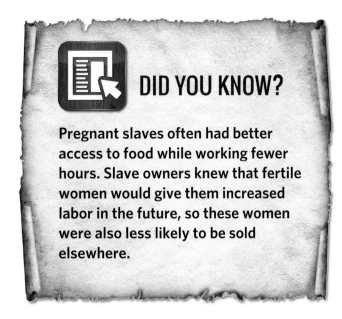

Some women were forced or **coerced** into sexual relationships for the sake of giving birth to babies that the owner could then use as slaves in the future. Selective breeding was not as common as one might think, however. The idea of "breeding slaves" was also a response to the 1807 decision to ban the slave trade by Congress. This decision, in addition to the high mortality rate for slaves, limited the number of slaves in the United States, so slave owners felt they needed to encourage slaves to reproduce. As an incentive, some slave owners promised freedom to women who produced a specific number of slaves. Whether or not these women ever achieved that freedom remains a mystery.

Motherhood was a difficult process, even when a child was able to stay on the same property as his parents. For example, a domestic slave might be called to nurse the babies of her white mistress, forced to neglect the feeding of her own children as a result. In fact, motherhood was so difficult for slaves that they feared the pain they would see inflicted on their children. Harriet Jacobs wrote about her ailing son, "Alas, what mockery it is for a slave mother to try to pray back her dying child to life! Death is better than slavery."

Then, there were the children whose mothers were slaves but fathers were white men, perhaps an overseer or the slave owner himself. The fathers of these children rarely acknowledged them, creating a **matrifocal** family. These children were considered black and forced into slavery. One of the most well-known cases was that of President Thomas Jefferson and his slave, Sally Hemings. The advent of DNA testing was able to show that all of Sally's children belong to President Jefferson. Rather than acknowledge the parentage of these children, people simply referred to them as "the children of the plantation."

A CHILDHOOD IN SLAVERY

Young boys were often separated from their mothers and sold. Young girls were much more likely to stay with their mothers throughout childhood, but they too would eventually be sold.

Because families could be so easily separated, many plantations took on a **communal** parenting culture. As such,

 EXTENDED FAMILIES IN SLAVERY

The complex nature of relationships among slaves meant that many people had to sneak around to see their loved ones. In fact, some slaves would sneak to nearby plantations to visit their extended family members, risking harsh punishment in the process. Children might also be raised by distant relatives if their parents had been sold elsewhere. For slaves like Frederick Douglass who were raised by grandparents, these bonds were extremely important.

For those who had no biological family members in their quarters, slaves would seek to build relationships with those near to them. Many slaves picked up surrogate families who would help care for them. People were forced to look out for each other.

groups would take on the responsibility of caring for the children if they were working in the farms. On large plantations, elderly women deemed too old or too weak to work would be tasked with caring for the little ones.

DID YOU KNOW?

Meals on large plantations might be cooked by an elderly slave who was no longer able to work in the fields. All the food would be cooked in a large pan and the slaves would gather around at meal times to get their fill.

Children were expected to perform many duties as slaves. In their earliest years, they might help look after other children, fetch water for the field laborers, or perhaps even assist in the kitchen. Once the children were deemed old enough, they would work in the fields alongside the adults.

Since education was not even a dream for most slaves, most of the lessons slave children would be taught included how to perform job duties well and how to be an obedient person. Life lessons could be taught around a fire or meal at nighttime.

Additionally, children born into slavery were often much smaller than their white counterparts. Often, these children were weaned when they were just a few months old and then put on a diet of porridge. Soon enough, they would be ating soups, potatoes, and cornbread. Unfortunately, these children would experience many health issues as a result of the lack of protein, Vitamin D, calcium, and other nutrients. These health conditions included abdominal swelling, bowed legs, skin issues, and even more serious ailments. By adulthood, they tended to be much shorter than the average white person.

Children were not immune to the punishments their parents faced. A child could be whipped or forced to eat bugs found in the crops they produced. They could also be starved or otherwise neglected by their masters.

At the same time, owners and mistresses might rely on children for information about conversation topics in the slave quarters. For this reason, the masters might try to build loyalty among small children with gifts and other small tokens of favor. They hoped the child would tattle on the adults who cared for them. As a result, parents would focus as much time as possible on encouraging their children to be loyal to the slave communities in which they lived.

THE LIVING QUARTERS OF SLAVE FAMILIES

Slaves typically lived in small wooden shacks with dirt floors and little (if any) furniture. Conditions were nowhere near great. Families living inside the shacks would often use clothing, wood, or rags to build partitions down for privacy. Large groups of people would be packed inside a single building, all crowding each other and huddled up. Without wood floors or proper beds, the slaves would make places to sleep out of straw and rags. Solomon Northup described his bed as a long plank. His pillow was made of wood and he would sleep under a rough blanket.

Generally, food rations were distributed weekly by the slave owner or overseer. Food would typically include molasses, peas, lard, corn meal, flour, and may be some meat. Some slaves were allowed to grow their own vegetables, but this would be considered a luxury. Generally, these meals were high in fat and starch, not necessarily healthy. Grandy claims his mother used to seek out water from holes and puddles for her children. For food, she would gather berries, corn, and potatoes.

Ultimately, solace was difficult to find for slaves. Family provided some semblance of peace and familiarity, but even that was not a guarantee. It was hard to be happy when you could lose anything at any possible moment, and this was a reality slaves had to deal with each day.

TEXT-DEPENDENT QUESTIONS

1. Who tended to the births of slaves?
2. Which American president was widely known to have children who were slaves?
3. What decision did Congress make in 1807?

RESEARCH PROJECT

Harriet Jacobs and Frederick Douglass are two authors of popular slave narratives that shed light on the family life of slaves. Choose any slave narrative to study or research. Find five quotes that speak to the theme of family from this narrative. Then, analyze each quote and write two to three paragraphs describing what this quote tells us about the time period. How did slaves cope with family issues? What problems arose in a family? Were slaves able to find solace in family? Why or why not?

This magazine illustration from 1857 shows slaves celebrating Christmas, one of the few holidays when they did not have to work. The white plantation owners are pictured near the center of the rowdy group.

WINTER HOLYDAYS IN THE SOUTHERN STATES. PLANTATION FROLIC ON CHRISTMAS EVE. FOR DESCRIPTION SEE PAGE 62.

 # WORDS TO UNDERSTAND

While a **kinship** relationship typically refers to a blood or biological relationship, it can also reference a deep bond of any kind.

A member of the **gentry** class is somebody who is of high social status.

Propaganda is misleading or biased information used to promote a point of view, often involving politics.

Miscegenation refers to reproduction between two people of different races. In the antebellum period, miscegenation often referred to a slave woman having a white man's baby.

CHAPTER 4

Social Life on the Plantation

Relationships between slaves and other slaves differed significantly from the relationships slaves had with non-slaves, as you might imagine. In spite of the fact that slaves were forced to work between twelve and twenty hours each day, slaves often had rich and complex social lives.

Unfortunately, little is known about the specific social interactions slaves had. Most of the information available today is based on slave narratives and statements that have withstood the test of time. What we do know is that social interactions ran the gamut from extremely negative and terrifying to very positive and warm.

THE SOCIAL LIVES OF DOMESTIC SLAVES

Slaves who worked in houses were generally more likely to build complex relationships with their owners because they lived in such close proximity to each other. For instance, many domestic workers who were women worked as nannies. They would build close relationships with the white children they raised, no matter the **gentry** status of their young charges. The slaves who worked inside the home had an insider view of the social politics inside plantation homes.

The interactions between slaves and their masters significantly impacted the level of dependence the white masters had on their

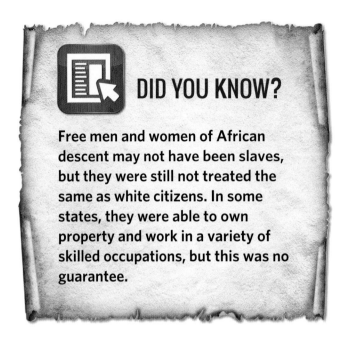

DID YOU KNOW?

Free men and women of African descent may not have been slaves, but they were still not treated the same as white citizens. In some states, they were able to own property and work in a variety of skilled occupations, but this was no guarantee.

slaves. Socializing with the masters and mistresses was often a heavy component of working as a domestic slave, especially in receiving orders. In spite of the frequency of social interaction between the white people and the slaves, little happened to influence the prejudice and bias masters and mistresses held onto.

This matter was made only more complicated by the fact that many of the slaves were related to the white people they served.

The relationship between domestic slaves and field slaves sometimes created some tension. Because domestic slaves were often given old clothing and other items their owners no longer wanted, field slaves might feel that domestic slaves received better treatment overall. On the other hand, slaves who worked in the fields might get one day off of work each week. This was often not the case for domestic slaves, who typically worked every day. As a result, a type of class system existed even amongst the slaves.

THE SOCIAL LIVES OF FIELD SLAVES

Kinship was an important facet of slave life, especially for those who worked in the fields. Even if individuals did not like each other, they had few others to turn to. Slaves living in these quarters were enduring the same treatment and lived through many of the same horrors. They could identify with each other.

Slaves who lived in quarters with other slaves could let their hair down at home. It was in the homes that slaves would gather

Wash day on the plantation: children tend the fire under a cauldron of hot water, while older slaves scrub the clothes.

to socialize, tell stories, and make plans. In fact, even the domestic workers might come to the quarters to provide news to the slaves regarding the house servants.

THE SOCIAL LIVES OF SLAVE CHILDREN

Children were the most likely people to build strong relationships outside of racial boundaries. White children and black children would often play together without much prejudice. Over time, this would change as the children adjusted to the systems society had put into place. As children became pre-teens, the slave children would experience much different lives, and they may even be forced to grow apart. Sometimes, the young slave children would go on to work for the children that had once been their playmates.

Most friendships among children were among slaves. Children would play with homemade toys, including marbles and wooden horses. They would create games to play without the luxuries afforded to white children, and sometimes they would sing songs with lyrics pertinent to their current situations. These childhood games made it somewhat easier to cope with a difficult life.

Children did not acknowledge their white fathers. In fact, few people ever acknowledged the role white men played in fathering slave children. As Harriet Jacobs wrote, "The secrets of slavery are concealed like those of the Inquisition. My master was, to my knowledge, the father of eleven slaves. But did the mothers dare to tell who was the father of their children? Did the other slaves dare to allude to it, except in whispers among themselves? No, indeed! They knew too well the terrible consequences."

WOMEN IN SLAVERY AND SOCIAL STATUS

In spite of the fact that life was quite different in America compared to Africa, slaves often still stuck to a system of male dominance. Slave women were often still living under the

Scan here to see what slave quarters looked like on a Louisiana plantation.

dominion of their husbands. At the same time, slave women were not treated with the same chivalry as white women in the outside world. For example, they were not allowed any semblance of modesty and were often forced to take off their clothing to be inspected by potential owners or to be punished in front of their peers. Women who refused to take off their clothing would be severely whipped.

Prevailing stereotypes and myths about slaves did nothing to help their cause. Southern literature and **propaganda** helped promote the idea of female slaves as sexually permissive. This propaganda was used to provide reason for the fact that so many slave women had given birth to children who clearly had white fathers. The women were painted in a negative light.

Additionally, many white people began to decry **miscegenation**, which they felt would damage the purity of races. Utah even passed a law that declared any slave who had sexual relations with a slave owner meant that the slave would be freed. Of course, this did not stop much of the abuse committed against women.

Ultimately, women faced many burdens in slavery that men did not. In addition to sexual abuse, they often worked earlier than the young boys. Girls could be found working in the homes of their mistresses before they turned eight. Harriet Jacobs wrote about her experience that at the age of six, she went to live in her mother's mistress in the big house where she would work. There, her mistress taught her how to read. When the mistress died, Harriet was sent to live with neglectful, abusive masters.

SOCIAL LIFE AWAY FROM HOME

State laws differed significantly. States like Alabama did not allow slaves to leave their master's property without written consent. Small groups would patrol the South and check the passes of anybody who appeared to be a slave. As a result, visiting other plantations would be extremely difficult in some regions. It was typically hard to socialize with those who did not live on the same plantation or farm without being sneaky.

Additionally, slave owners would try to limit exposure of their slaves to the outside world in general. They thought this would reduce the slave's chances of escape or rebellion because they would have fewer resources in the outside world. In doing this, slave owners also thought they could prevent slaves from dreaming or making goals. If slaves left the plantation without

POSITIVE INTERACTIONS WITH OWNERS

It would seem that some slaves had positive relationships with their owners, though this was not the norm. Samuel Williams, a former slave, wrote that one of his owners actually taught him to ride horses when he was a young boy. Williams said his owner even had a saddle made for him. Some slaves were trained to become horse jockeys and trainers, though Williams never became one.

Some slaves, like Frederick Douglass, were even taught to read by their owners. This was often in spite of laws in many states that expressly forbade the education of slaves.

Even some of the positive social interactions and graces bestowed upon slaves were a form of manipulation. For instance, after the international slave trade was abolished, some slave owners improved living conditions so that they would not feel compelled to escape.

It is important to keep in mind that in spite of some of these experiences, enslaved people were subject to the horrors of slavery, including punishment. These positive interactions did little to improve the conditions of slavery.

permission, they would likely be lashed.

Some slave codes also called for slaves not to be allowed to leave a plantation unless they were accompanied by a white person. Any potential slave seen outside the plantation allowed could be chastised by every white person he or she encountered.

FEARS OF REBELLION INFLUENCED WHITE INTERACTIONS

Over time, white slave owners feared that their slaves would rise up in rebellion against them. Not only did this encourage slave owners to prohibit reading and education for slaves, but it also impacted the way slaves were allowed to socialize with each other. A level of mistrust might arise between slaves who thought the other might reveal information to the masters.

Additionally, slave owners and overseers might decide that they needed to assert dominance over their slaves. Public humiliation, shackling, whipping, branding, and mutilation were sometimes the main social interactions slaves had with white people. Sexual abuse of women was also part of this mistreatment.

Pregnant women were not immune to these punishments. Moses Grandy described an experience in which, "one of [his] sisters was so severely punished . . . that labour was brought on, and the child born in the field. This very overseer, Mr. Brooks, killed in this manner a girl named Mary. . ." The white men were never criminally charged with crimes related to acts like these. In fact, slaves were not even considered people unless they were the ones who committed crimes.

Sometimes punishments were doled out simply because a slave had "sassed" a white person. As such, slaves had to be careful about the ways they interacted with white people, even if they were not slave owners themselves. Even the children of slave owners were allowed to whip and otherwise punish slaves for small slights.

Slave owners felt that they could produce the perfect slave by ordering discipline and submission through instilling a sense

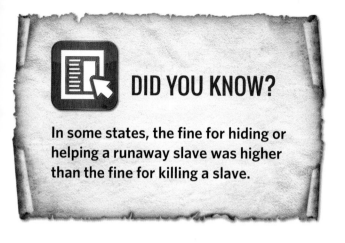

of inferiority and fear among slaves. Slave owners perceived brutality as the best means of achieving this goal. For example, punishment did not necessarily end with a whipping. In some cases, the overseers would order others to rub substances like red pepper into the wounds of the slaves, aggravating the injuries. All of these punishments would be done in public to set an example to other slaves, almost as if to say, "This could be you. Don't step out of line."

Even the few anti-cruelty laws some states passed did little to calm the harsh interactions between slaves and their owners. The 1740 South Carolina law prohibiting cruelty to slaves merely prevented slaves from certain types of mutilation, including scalding, amputations, and burning. Additionally, those who owned slaves could be fined if they did not punish runaway slaves returned to them. This gave slave owners even more incentive to treat these men and women poorly.

SOCIAL INTERACTIONS IN SLAVERY

Social interactions had to be strategic for those who endured slavery. Slaves had to watch what they said around anybody they did not trust. Ultimately, slaves were viewed as outsiders in the world they lived in, in spite of the fact that they or their ancestors had been unwillingly brought to the Americas in the first place.

It would be impossible to simplify the types of interactions slaves had with each other and with others. Being on high alert for potential social and physical missteps was critical, and it surely affected each person mentally and physically.

TEXT-DEPENDENT QUESTIONS

1. Why did domestic and field slaves have different relationships with their masters?

2. Why did slave owners not want their slaves to leave their plantations or farms?

3. Which slaves were more likely to have relationships that crossed racial boundaries?

RESEARCH PROJECT

Choose a field or domestic slave to research, paying close attention to the social life the slave may have had. Write a one-page paper about the slave's social life, and try to use one or two quotes to support your claims. How does this social life compare to one he or she may have had today?

 WORDS TO UNDERSTAND

A **lamentation** is typically an impassioned expression of grief or sorrow. A song that is a lamentation is typically sad.

In folklore, **tricksters** are characters who outsmart others. In African folktales, Br'er Rabbit is a common trickster.

The **status quo** refers to the existing state of affairs, the way things are. Status quo typically refers to social and political situations.

CHAPTER 5

Customs of the Plantation

Slave communities turned to music, entertainment, and other customs to cope with some of the horrors of the society in which they were thrust into. Slaves often built their own customs, which were often a combination of cultural components from Africa melded with American life. They had to build on to the components of African culture available to them in North America, establishing brand new customs.

Many of the customs slaves established in the South during this time period relied on providing comfort and solace. Culture became a type of coping mechanism for those who had few options and nowhere else to turn.

EDUCATION FOR SLAVES

Generally speaking, education was not allowed for slaves. In fact, some states punished anybody teaching slaves to read or write with fines and jail time. The first state to pass laws against slave education were passed in South Carolina in 1740, and they dictated that slaves would not be allowed to write. Georgia passed a similar law less than twenty years later. After Nat Turner's slave rebellion in 1831, the laws spread like wildfire. For example, Mississippi soon passed laws requiring all freed African Americans to leave the state out of fear that they would educate slaves.

However, all of these laws did not mean that slaves were never

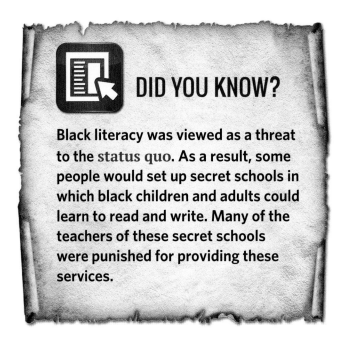

DID YOU KNOW?

Black literacy was viewed as a threat to the status quo. As a result, some people would set up secret schools in which black children and adults could learn to read and write. Many of the teachers of these secret schools were punished for providing these services.

educated. Slaves could learn a lot from each other, even beyond the basic subjects of reading and writing. Slaves could learn from their parents, family members, or fellow slaves they developed a kinship with. In some cases, masters and overseers would step in to provide education for slaves. In some cases, the purpose for these lessons was for religious instruction. Slave owners wanted their slaves to be able to read the Bible. Sometimes, the lessons had a more practical purpose. Slaves who knew basic math or reading could assist their masters with skills like record-keeping.

For all too many slaves, spending time on education was simply not practical. Children who worked outside in the fields for long hours at a time had very little access to indoor education time. They could not focus on studies.

Even for those living outside the confines of slavery in the 1700s, education was hard to come by for those who were not white. Black people living in the northern states were the most likely to be formally educated. The Quakers played a significant role in spreading education among free black Americans, but lack of support and financial hardship played a role in making education less accessible to those who needed it. After President Abraham Lincoln abolished slavery following the Civil War, segregation and lack of resources still made it difficult for former slaves to attend school.

In spite of difficulties learning to read and write, slaves did learn how to tell their stories. Slave narratives were written or dictated by slaves and former slaves throughout the eighteenth and nineteenth centuries. They revealed significant details about the time they spent in captivity. These slave narratives would become important as time pressed on because they showed that slaves were speaking out against their treatment. They were not silent about the inhumanity they faced on a daily basis, and they had not given up their identities. They simply had few choices.

CRAFTS AND CREATIVITY IN SLAVERY

Crafts became a significant part of slave life. Slaves might learn how to weave baskets, make fishing nets, or create musical instruments. In spite of the heavy workload assigned to slaves, they could find ways to become creative after they had put in their hours.

Handmade sweetgrass baskets woven in the Gullah (West African) style typical of the South Carolina low country.

Additionally, slaves would use local materials to create objects similar to those they had used in Africa. These could include combs, seats, ceramic pieces, and even entire canoes. They would rely on many of the same patterns and techniques that had once been popular in Africa. Slaves would incorporate joyous patterns and themes into practical items, promoting at least a bit of happiness in their blankets, baskets, pipes, and rugs.

SLAVE STORYTELLING

With reading and writing an impossibility for many slaves, oral traditions were an important part of their culture. Slaves would pass on songs, prayers, and stories by repeating them to younger generations. Oral traditions were one of the only ways slaves in America could build cultural connections to their African heritage.

Storytelling involved folktales, especially those involving tricksters. Br'er Rabbit, like other hares and rabbits in African folklore, have been portrayed as tricksters. Br'er Rabbit was an animal who learned how to outwit other animals in crafty, unique ways. The rabbit was often the hero in the stories he is featured in, but he was also considered an amoral character with good and bad facets. While the trickster is not a figure anybody would aspire to become, his stories revolve around survival and doing one's best to get by with the circumstances they have been handed.

These stories served the purpose of promoting creativity but also helped the teller fantasize about getting out of their current circumstances. Like many other forms of creativity during this time, storytelling offered one way to cope with a life in slavery.

Some slaves had been trained as artisans as part of their work, and they could use these skills in their personal lives as well. For example, many slaves learned how to use wrought iron to decorate with and to use for other practical purposes. Blacksmiths could use their skills to create practical and spiritual items out of the iron.

Pottery was also a useful skill among slaves, who would make bowls and jugs. Some of these items were also used during the burial process when slaves paid respects to their deceased loved ones.

Textiles were also crucial for slaves, and many had the skills necessary to weave and spin so that they could create clothing and quilts for their communities. Some slaves would even make clothing and blankets for slaveholders.

SLAVE MUSIC

Music did become a major component of slave life. Slaves would use gourds they had grown to make music. They could also use sea shells, wood, bones, and string to make their own banjos, bells, drums, fiddles, and other musical instruments. But one of the most popular instruments for slaves was the human voice.

At the time, the most important songs among slaves were known as "spirituals." Slaves would often sing these songs in the fields as they worked. Those who supported or benefited from slavery would use these songs as evidence that slaves were happy to work. Seemingly, they had not heard the lyrics of the songs, which included discussion of the pain of not seeing their families as well as hope for slavery to end. Spirituals were often call-and-response songs that allowed for large groups to create melodies together. Often the songs were improvised.

Frederick Douglass described the music in his narrative. "This they would sing, as a chorus, to words which to many would seem unmeaning jargon, but which, nevertheless, were full of meaning to themselves. I have sometimes thought that the mere hearing of those songs would do more to impress some minds with the horrible character of slavery, than the reading of whole volumes of philosophy on the subject could do."

One form of singing occurred in the form of "shouts," which occurred when the slaves would stand in a circle while dancing or chanting. Many of the chants were those of **lamentation**, sorrow, and protest. These meetings of emotional expression were a strong outlet for individuals living in slavery, and they could often hide the true messages of the songs to avoid detection by white slave owners and masters. Jeanette Murphy stated,

> During my childhood my observations were centered upon a few very old negroes who came directly from Africa, and upon many others whose parents were African born, and I early came to the conclusion, based upon negro authority, that the greater part of the music, their methods, their scale, their type of thought, their dancing, their patting of feet, their clapping of hands, their grimaces and pantomime, and their gross superstitions came straight from Africa.

Slaves like Solomon Northup used music to explore their pain. He wrote, "If it had not been for my beloved violin, I scarcely can conceive how I could have endured the long years of bondage. It was my companion—the friend of my bosom—triumphing loudly

Scan here to listen to "Swing Low, Sweet Chariot," a spiritual.

when I was joyful, and uttering its soft melodious consolations when I was sad."

At one point, slave owners and overseers began to see drum beats as a threat. They thought the drums could help signal an uprising among the slaves, so they started banning drums for slaves. In 1739, the state of South Carolina prohibited drums for slaves.

Music produced during the days of antebellum slavery had a lasting impact on the landscape of pop culture. In fact, the music slaves created directly paved the way for gospel, jazz, and blues music in the future.

THE POOR HEALTH OF SOUTHERN SLAVES

Unfortunately, slaves lived with unsanitary conditions that were only made worse by the fact that the South's heat and humidity were relentless. These weather conditions could lead to heat exhaustion, heat stroke, sunburn, and other ailments.

When it came to medical care for slaves, treatment was limited. Slaves had little medical knowledge, and even professional doctors had few resources during this time period compared to the availability of medical treatment in America today. Generally, other slaves provided medical care to each other. They often learned these skills from older slaves.

Sometimes, slaves used folk remedies from Africa as a means of treating illness and wounds. They would also build new remedies based on the plants and herbs available to them in America. The use of herbal medicines could also be used to gain favor with slave owners. Slaves who had expertise in midwifery or

Slaves used many different herbs, roots, barks, and spices for their medicinal effects. Burdock root had antibiotic and anti-inflammatory properties.

Interior of a slave's quarters on a plantation in Louisiana.

nursing could be called upon to treat the masters and mistresses in the plantation house. On the other hand, slaves could also use knowledge of medicines and herbs to resist slavery by poisoning owners and livestock.

If a slave was in the type of shape that might require a medical physician, the slave owners would often first try to heal the slaves themselves or with the help of their wives. This would be an attempt to save money. If the ailment was something a doctor could treat at home, the master or mistress may call his or her own doctor to make a house call.

When slaves did go to the hospital, they might not see the same doctor that treated whites. Some physicians believed that the bodies of white and black people were different. Additionally, because the lives of slaves weren't considered important, they might be used for experimental treatments that could be fatal.

FOOD IN THE SLAVE QUARTERS

Inadequate nutrition also made life more difficult for slaves, making them more susceptible to illness. While some slaves had plenty of access to food, many others did not. Rations were more common, and food was often passed out weekly by the masters or overseers. If the slave's owners had fallen on hard times and had difficulty securing food for their own family, the slaves would suffer even more. Still, the slaves did the best they could with the foods they were given, and they sometimes had the ability to grow and produce their own.

Pork was the primary meat for plantations at the time, when slaves did have access to meat. Maintaining pigs was easier than maintaining cows, and the meat could be preserved in a simpler fashion. But one problem arose with the increase in pork and decrease in beef: lack of milk for people who were working all day, nearly every day.

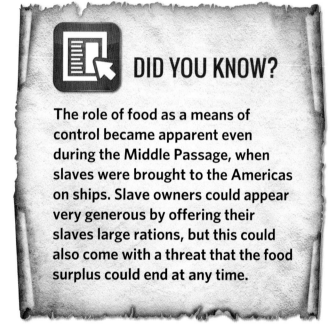

DID YOU KNOW?

The role of food as a means of control became apparent even during the Middle Passage, when slaves were brought to the Americas on ships. Slave owners could appear very generous by offering their slaves large rations, but this could also come with a threat that the food surplus could end at any time.

Corn also became a significant part of a slave's diet. Corn was readily available because it could grow better on less fertile lands than other crops. Slaves would soon learn how to make cornbread using this abundant ration. Making this dish was so simple that even the children could do it.

Greens were another staple in the slave diet. Collard greens and kale were popular vegetables available in the South. The slaves would boil the greens and add some bacon or pork fat for flavor. Greens were easy to cook, especially for large groups of workers with few resources.

Sweet potatoes were another staple in antebellum slave culture, especially because they were such hearty vegetables that could grow in difficult conditions. Yams had been plentiful in western Africa, and Native Americans had been using sweet potatoes for many years. The sweet potatoes were often roasted in leaves for flavor.

Ultimately, the food the slaves ate were based on a fusion of African cultural staples and the availability of resources in the Americas.

SLAVE CLOTHING IN THE SOUTH

Another reason why slaves suffered from so many injuries and illnesses was the lack of clothing and shoes. Initially, slaves had been given European clothing that they were not used to. The European-style clothing was made of material inferior to the material used for the slaveholders' clothing.

Sometimes, slaves were simply given material and expected to create their own clothing. Men and boys were given cotton material for shirts and pants. Heavier denim may have been given for winter jeans. Women would use their allotted material to create shifts, petticoats, and gowns. Blanket cloth would be used to make a coat. The slaves would also be issued shoes, but these did not tend to last long. Slaves who worked inside might not even receive a coat.

Slaves were forced to build identity in a new place and in terrible circumstances. Regardless of the difficulties they faced, slaves worked with what they were given to make the best possible lives for themselves. They were forced to become resourceful survivors, and they built a culture for themselves in the process.

TEXT-DEPENDENT QUESTIONS

1. Why was corn so readily available to slaves?
2. Why might a slaveholder want a slave to learn to read or write?
3. Which state banned drums, and why?

RESEARCH PROJECT

Choose a component of slave culture, like food, clothing, education, or music, to research. Find quotes by at least three former slaves from autobiographies, memoirs, or slave narratives. Based on these quotes, create a presentation in which you teach your class about this aspect of culture and why these customs may have developed in the first place.

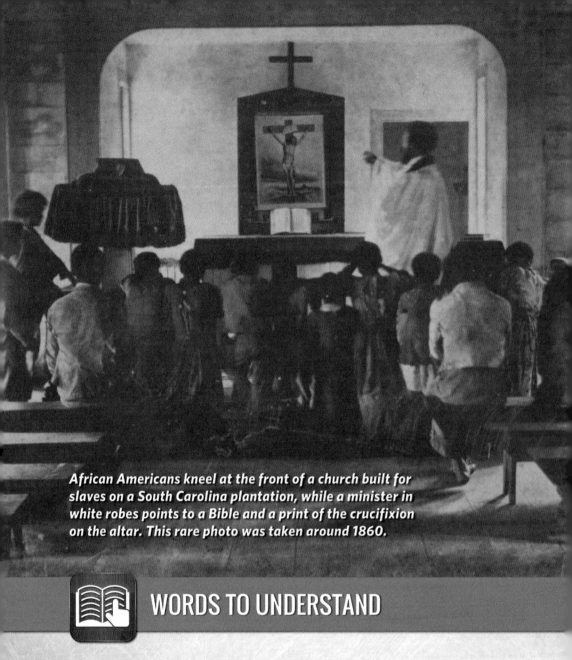

African Americans kneel at the front of a church built for slaves on a South Carolina plantation, while a minister in white robes points to a Bible and a print of the crucifixion on the altar. This rare photo was taken around 1860.

WORDS TO UNDERSTAND

Myalism was a Jamaican folk religion that focused on ancestral power. The religion involved dancing, drumming, sacrifice, and herbs.

A **benevolent** action is one that is kind or well-meaning.

If you have **ambivalent** feelings about something, you feel contradictory or have mixed feelings about it.

CHAPTER 6

Slavery and Religion

For slaves, religion became a blend of African religions and Christianity. Slaves came from cultures practicing many religions. While some slaves may have practiced Islam, others followed Christianity when they arrived in the United States. Slaves incorporated elements of African religions into their Christianity sometimes too. Religion was by no means static or identical among slaves in America.

Frank Cannon detailed his experience, writing, "Our master built us a church in our quarters and sent his preacher to preach to us. He was a white preacher. Said he wanted his slaves to be Christians." Slave masters had a significant influence on their slaves and the religious options available to them, but slaves were also resourceful with their religious worship.

THE ROLE OF RELIGION FOR SLAVES

Religion provided solace, inspiration, and motivation for slaves. Religious worship provided something to look forward too. It provided slaves with meaning and some semblance of joy. Worship was stability, and it was crucial to the emotional well-being of slaves to be able to attend services, even if these services were in their own homes.

Of course, religion had also been used to justify slavery. The Baptist church in the South was a major proponent of slavery, primarily for economic and social purposes. In the North, Baptists claimed that one race could not be held superior to another, but the southern Baptists claimed that God had reason to separate the races. The Baptist church split up after the church made a ruling that those who held slaves were not eligible to have funds for mission work. The South developed its own form of the Baptist religion as a result.

Catholicism was largely **ambivalent** about the concept of slavery for many years in the South, up until the dawn of the Civil War. Catholicism did not have a significant hold on the United States until the 1840s, and most of the slaveholders in the South were Protestants. In 1839, the Pope issued a statement declaring the slave trade was wrong, but many Catholics did not interpret the statement as being anti-slavery as a whole. As a result, bishops in the United States did not speak against slavery. At the same time, Mexico (which was a Catholic country) did not allow slavery.

Slaves understood the hypocrisy of religion as well. William Wells Brown wrote, "Their child-robbing, man-stealing, woman-whipping, chain-forging, marriage-destroying, slave-manufacturing, man-slaying religion, will not be received as genuine; and the people of the free states cannot expect to live in union with slaveholders, without becoming contaminated with slavery." He saw through their beliefs and determined that as long as slavery existed, it would influence American life for all.

Religion developed within the societal structure of slavery too,

DID YOU KNOW?

Religion could also bring domestic and field slaves together. Slaves who usually did not fraternize would have reason to come together for worship purposes, building kinship between the two groups.

RELIGIOUS ANTI-SLAVERY MOVEMENTS

The Society of Friends, also known as Quakers, were one of the few religious groups that did not support slavery. Quakers in Pennsylvania declared their opposition to slavery as early as 1688. Quakers continued speaking out against slavery during and after the American War for Independence. In the 1770s, many Quakers joined the Pennsylvania Abolition Society, a group formed to advocate for an end to slavery.

The development of the Underground Railroad gave Quakers another way to get involved in abolition. Many Quakers participated, helping people escape the confines of slavery. A Quaker named Levi Coffin was so active in this secret group that he was nicknamed the "president of the Underground Railroad."

This is not to say that all Quakers were against slavery. Quaker beliefs were diverse, and some members of the Society of Friends were quick to express pro-slavery sentiment. A few Quakers actually traded slaves as a business and argued that slavery was actually a benevolent cause.

Methodists were also against slavery, and they were at the forefront of the abolition movement. In fact, Methodists established several organizations that helped to free slaves, including the American Colonization Society. This group arranged for freed slaves to establish a colony in West Africa that today is the country of Liberia. Methodist preachers called the practice of slavery immoral and evil.

Still, some Methodists did own slaves. The church split in 1850, and some southern Methodist churches supported slavery until after the Civil War.

After the Emancipation Proclamation went into effect in 1863, the African Methodist Episcopal Church welcomed former slaves and even taught them to read and write.

This was an Episcopal church attended by slaves on the Rockville plantation near Charleston, South Carolina, built in 1858. (The interior of the building is pictured on page 58.)

and not only to benefit the slaves. Baptist and Methodist ministers even began to change the messaging of their sermons to ensure that they could accommodate slavery within their religions. Rather than use Christianity as a way to eliminate slavery, the preachers might suggest that masters treat their slaves better. While preachers often identified the personhood of slaves, they often still emphasized their role of property too.

This had an alienating effect on many slaves. Because Christianity was used so often to justify slavery, some slaves rejected Christianity altogether and sought out their own perspectives. These slaves might focus on stories from the New Testament as well as the stories in the Old Testament about Moses leading slaves out of Egypt. The Book of Exodus became especially important among slave preachers.

For many men and women who were slaves, religion gave them a sense of peace. It is easy to see the allure of religion for slaves who had endured terrible hardships. Perhaps they would be able to see their children again in the afterlife. If they were obedient in this life, perhaps they would be rewarded in the afterlife. Slaves had a variety of reasons to hold faith, even if they felt they'd been given more than their fair share to deal with in life itself.

THE PERCEIVED THREAT OF RELIGION TO SLAVEHOLDERS

Slaves were often prohibited from meeting in groups unless the purpose of the meeting was for worship. After the 1831 rebellion of Nat Turner, some states even began to put restrictions on those meetings. The rebellion may have been partly inspired by an 1829 text by African-American abolitionist David Walker titled "An Appeal to the Coloured Citizens of the World." The text condemned pro-slavery Christians and called for slaves to revolt. Out of fear that other slaves would be inspired to rise up, some states began to require that congregations of slaves would require a white overseer to ensure the sermons were not rebellious or promoting violence against slaveholders.

To learn how the Fugitive Slave Act of 1850 made it harder for slaves to escape, scan here.

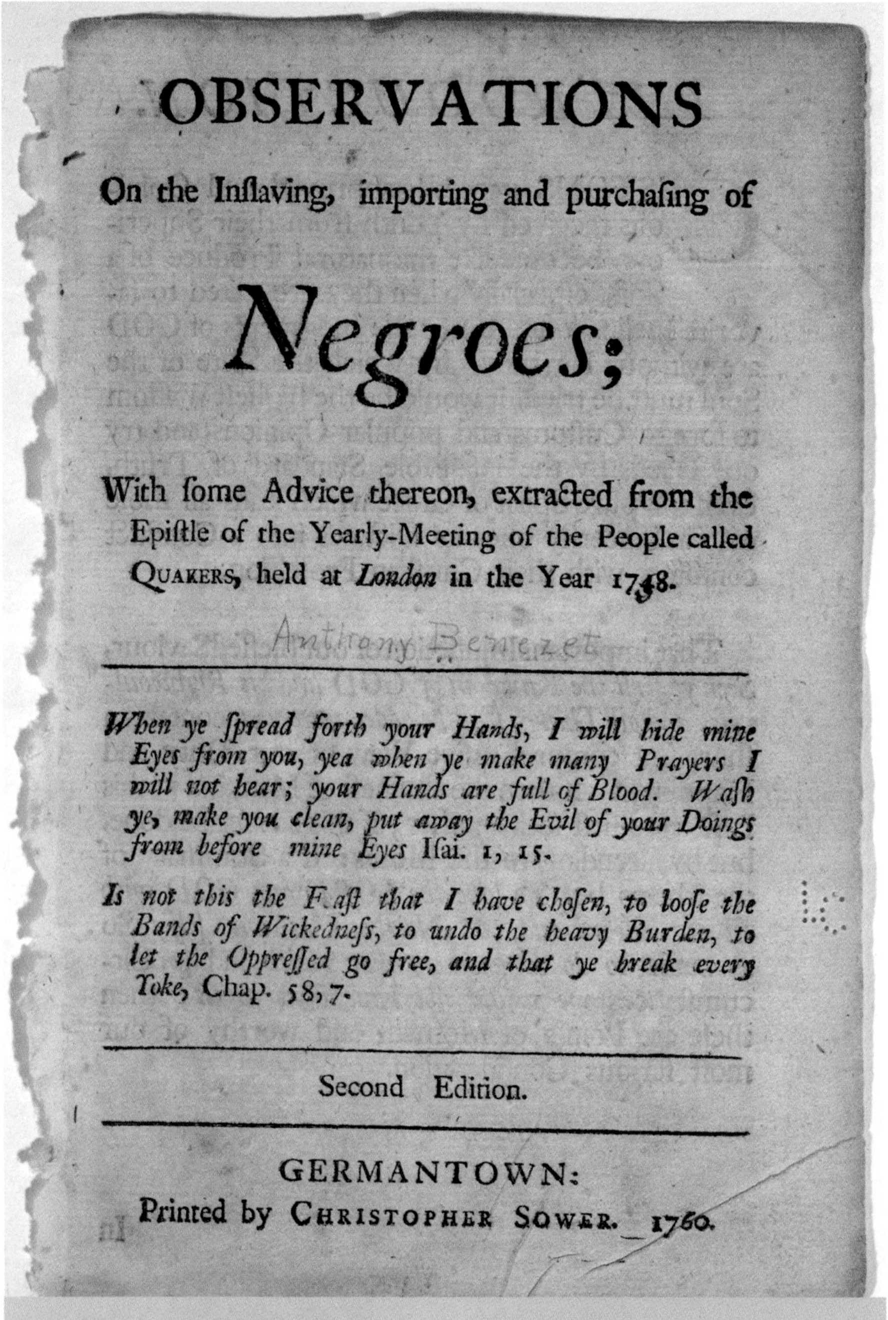

OBSERVATIONS

On the Inslaving, importing and purchasing of

Negroes;

With some Advice thereon, extracted from the Epistle of the Yearly-Meeting of the People called QUAKERS, held at *London* in the Year 1748.

Anthony Benezet

When ye spread forth your Hands, I will hide mine Eyes from you, yea when ye make many Prayers I will not hear; your Hands are full of Blood. Wash ye, make you clean, put away the Evil of your Doings from before mine Eyes Isai. 1, 15.

Is not this the Feast that I have chosen, to loose the Bands of Wickedness, to undo the heavy Burden, to let the Oppressed go free, and that ye break every Yoke, Chap. 58, 7.

Second Edition.

GERMANTOWN:

Printed by CHRISTOPHER SOWER. 1760.

First page of a 1760 anti-slavery book by Anthony Benezet, one of the first American abolitionists. Benezet, a Quaker from the Philadelphia area, founded one of the world's first anti-slavery organizations in 1775.

Due to fears of slave uprisings, many Southern slaves would attend white churches with their masters, typically sitting in back of the church. The slaves would hear the preacher discussing topics perhaps more pertinent to the lives of white people, and they may have had difficulty identifying with the messages that called for quiet subservience from laborers.

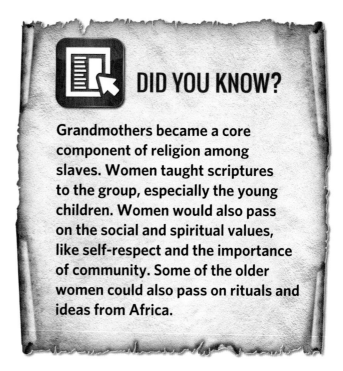

DID YOU KNOW?

Grandmothers became a core component of religion among slaves. Women taught scriptures to the group, especially the young children. Women would also pass on the social and spiritual values, like self-respect and the importance of community. Some of the older women could also pass on rituals and ideas from Africa.

Some slave owners did not want their slaves to become Christians at all, because some writings in the Bible said that all people are equal before God. This was also part of the reason that plantation owners did not allow slaves to learn how to read.

Very early on, some laws had established that slaves could not be baptized. They could not be held as slaves if they were. Laws regarding the Christianity of slaves were vague, however, and they fell to the wayside. After 1706, most states had passed their own laws stating that a person's religious beliefs would not impact their status as slaves.

Charles Spurgeon had been a famous preacher in England, but Southern plantation owners were unhappy with his anti-slavery statements. His teachings were burned out of fear that anti-slavery sentiment would spread through the South.

In fact, some white Christians joined groups that promoted slavery and racial disparity. One such group was known as the

The Reverend Theodore S. Wright was an African-American minister in a Presbyterian church in New York City. In the 1830s, he helped to establish the American Anti-Slavery Society (AASS), which mailed pamphlets and informational material about the horrors of slavery throughout the United States.

Ku Klux Klan, a group that promoted violence against African Americans. The group gained prominence in the 1860s, as tensions surrounding slavery came to a head.

Christianity as a form of social control was evident to many slaves, but this does not mean many slaves did not welcome the religion as a form of solace. In fact, some slaves built worship areas in their communities for visiting preachers to speak; however, they still maintained awareness that religious messages were useful in swaying beliefs and promoting dangerous notions, including the idea that slaves should be happily subservient.

CHANGING RELIGION

Coming to the Americas was not the first exposure to Christianity for many Africans. In fact, Portuguese missionaries had gone to Africa in the 1400s in the hopes of converting new Christians. As a result, some of the slaves who came to the United States already had some semblance of Christianity in their lives.

Some slaves would go on to derive components of African religions to establish their faiths. They would use components of voodoo and **myalism**, for example. Slaves who came directly from Africa would utilize components of several religions sometimes, especially if they were forced into Christianity by their owners. For example, slaves might use the cross as a religious symbol, but they might wear it as a means of warding off spirits they thought might harm them.

The fusion of religions brought about unique pockets of religion for slaves. For example, slaves living in Louisiana tended more toward fusing Christianity and voodoo. One component of religious fusion meant that many aspects of life became sacred. Even secular events, like work or cooking, became affiliated with religion.

This drawing from 1835 shows a southerner mob illegally sorting through mail to find and destroy abolitionist literature. The sign "$20,000 Reward for Tappan" refers to an offer made by plantation owners in New Orleans for the capture of abolitionist Arthur Tappan, president of the AASS. When mailings to the South were blocked, the AASS had to find other ways to get their anti-slavery message to the people.

One form of religion, known as Conjure, which came from West Central African ideas about nature and spirituality merging. Conjure promoted the idea that nature and spirituality could be used for good or bad, but it could ultimately be healing and nurturing with certain practices requiring roots and herbs.

For those slaves who practiced Islam, staying connected to their roots could be a difficult experience. Slaves especially struggled to preserve the Arabic language throughout the generations, which was especially true if they opted to convert to Christianity in America.

Some slaves actually began creating their own religious holidays and observances, continuing to meet together in secret. On large plantations with many slaves, the groups would meet in the middle of the night. Since slaves typically only had one day off each week, they have very little time to develop religious structure and hold worship services amongst themselves.

And in spite of the progress of the churches and religious beliefs of the slaves, problems of bias persisted. For example, women might not be ordained as preachers. This became a problem for the Methodist church when women like Jarena Lee claimed they had the right to preach. The African Methodist Episcopal Zion church allowed women to become ordained before many other churches.

Religion was also complex in the northern states. As black churches were established in the United States, they had a few distinct qualities. They incorporate different songs and types of music. The music was rhythmic and used dancing and beats as part of worship.

Ultimately, one of the biggest benefits of religion was bringing a sense of community to slaves who were struggling with the challenges of life. Religion was one of the biggest coping mechanisms for those suffering in slavery.

TEXT-DEPENDENT QUESTIONS

1. Which religions were largely anti-slavery?
2. What did Levi Coffin lead?
3. What text did David Walker write?

RESEARCH PROJECT

Choose one of the religions slaves practiced in the United States, even if it is not mentioned in this chapter. What beliefs did this religion have about slavery, and how did it justify this position? What leaders were involved in expressing this belief or trying to change it? How did this belief change during and after the Civil War and Emancipation Proclamation? Write an essay in which you answer these questions and describe the religious repercussions of this belief for the slaves.

SERIES GLOSSARY OF KEY TERMS

antebellum period—refers to the period from 1789, after the United States became an independent nation, until the Civil War began in 1861.

aristocracy—the highest class in a society.

cash crop—a crop, such as cotton or tobacco, that is produced primarily for sale at a market. Cultivation of cash crops was very labor-intensive, and required large numbers of slaves.

chattel slavery—a type of slavery in which the enslaved person becomes the personal property (chattel) of the owner and can be bought, sold, or inherited. The person is a slave for life, and their offspring are also enslaved.

domestic slave trade—the buying, selling, and transportation of enslaved people within a territory or country, such as the United States or the Spanish colonies.

Emancipation Proclamation—a presidential proclamation issued in late 1862 that declared that all African-Americans held as slaves in rebellious states during the Civil War would be considered free by the United States government on January 1, 1863.

indentured servants—a form of servitude in which a person agrees to work in exchange for food and shelter for a certain period of time.

Middle Passage—name for the slave trade route from Africa to America across the Atlantic Ocean, which was infamous due to its horrific conditions.

overseer—a plantation manager who supervised the work activities of slaves.

Quaker—a member of the Religious Society of Friends, a Christian group that was strongly opposed to slavery.

segregation—the separation of people in their daily lives based on race.

sharecropper—a tenant farmer in the South who was given credit by the landowner to pay for seeds, tools, living quarters, and food, in exchange for a share of his crop at the time of harvesting.

tenant farmer—a person who farms on rented land.

transatlantic slave trade—the capturing, enslaving, buying, selling, and transportation of Africans across the Atlantic to the Americas.

Underground Railroad—term for the route used by runaway slaves to reach freedom, either in the Northern states or Canada.

white supremacy—a belief that white people are superior to people of all other races, especially the black race, and should therefore dominate society.

slave codes—laws passed in the South to restrict the activity of slaves. Some laws made it illegal to teach slaves how to read or write. Others prevented slaves from moving freely from place to place without a pass, or from holding religious services without the presence of a white man to monitor their activities.

p. 13   "No man can put a chain..." Frederick Douglass, Speech at the Civil Rights Mass-Meeting Held at Lincoln Hall (1883). Reprinted at Teaching American History, accessed February 17, 2019. http://teachingamericanhistory.org/library/document/the-civil-rights-case/.

p. 14   "The midnight sky and the..." Frederick Douglass, quoted in Bradford, Sarah, *Scenes in the Life of Harriet Tubman* (Auburn: W.J. Moses, Printer, 1869), p. 7.

p. 18   "Our drink was the water..." Moses Grandy, *Narrative of the Life of Moses Grandy; Late a Slave in the United States of America* (London: C. Gilpin, 1843), p. 26.

p. 18   "A strap is fastened to it..." Solomon Northup, *Twelve Years a Slave: Narrative of Solomon Northup* (New York: Miller, Orton, and Mulligan, 1855), p. 165.

p. 19   "The overseer stood with his watch..." Moses Grandy, *Narrative*, p. 27.

p. 19   "One black man is kept..." Moses Grandy, *Narrative*, p. 27.

p. 21   "A city slave is almost..." Frederick Douglass, *Narrative of the Life of Frederick Douglass, an American Slave* (Boston: Anti-Slavery Office, 1849), p. 34.

p. 27   "The slave girl had to be..." Frank D. Banks, *Plantation Courtship, The Journal of American Folklore* 7, no. 25 (Apr-Jun 1894), p. 147.

p. 28   "For, all the regulations on..." Presbyterian Synod of Kentucky, as quoted in Ivan E. McDougle, *The Journal of Negro History* Vol. 3, No. 3 (1918), pp. 288. Reprinted at JSTOR, accessed February 17, 2019. https://www.jstor.org/stable/2713411.

p. 28   "Brothers and sister, parents..." McDougle, *The Journal of Negro History*, pp. 288.

p. 30   "My mother often hid us…" Moses Grandy, *Narrative*, p. 8.

p. 31   "Alas, what mockery it is…" Harriet A. Jacobs, *Incidents in the Life of a Slave Girl, Written by Herself* (Boston: Thayer and Eldridge, 1861).

p. 40   "The secrets of slavery are…" Jacobs, *Incidents in the Life of a Slave Girl.*

p. 43   "One of [his] sisters was…" Moses Grandy, *Narrative*, p. 28.

p. 51   "This they would sing…" Frederick Douglass, *Narrative of the Life of Frederick Douglass, an American Slave*, p. 13.

p. 51   "During my childhood my observations…" Jeanette Murphy, "The Survival of African Music in America," *Popular Science Monthly*, Vol. 55 (1899).

p. 51   "If it had not been…" Solomon Northup, *Twelve Years a Slave: Narrative of Solomon Northup*, p. 217.

p. 59   "Our master built us…" Frank Cannon, *Federal Writers' Project: Slave Narrative Project*, Vol. 2, Arkansas, Part 2, Cannon-Evans. (1936). Reprinted at Library of Congress, accessed February 19, 2019, https://www.loc.gov/item/mesn022/.

p. 61   "Their child-robbing, man-stealing…" William Wells Brown, *From Fugitive Slave to Free Man: The Autobiographies of William Wells Brown*. (Columbia: University of Missouri Press, 1993). p. 88.

FURTHER READING

Aleckson, Sam. *Before the War, and After the Union: An Autobiography*. Boston: Gold Mind, 1929.

Call, Charles. *Fifty Years in Chains; Or, The Life of an American Slave*. New York: H. Dayton, 1859.

Camp, Stephanie. *Closer to Freedom: Enslaved Women and Everyday Resistance in the Plantation South*. Chapel Hill, NC: The University of North Carolina Press, 2004.

Carey, Brycchan. *From Peace to Freedom: Quaker Rhetoric and the Birth of American Antislavery, 1658–1761*. New Haven, CT: Yale University Press, 2012.

Davis, David Brion. *The Problem of Slavery in Western Culture*. New York: Oxford University Press, 2008.

Morrison, Toni. *Beloved*. New York: Alfred A. Knopf, 1987.

Ruiz, Dorothy. *Amazing Grace: African American Grandmothers as Caregivers and Conveyors of Traditional Value*. Westport, CT: Praeger, 2004.

Thomas, Hugh. *The Slave Trade: The Story of the Atlantic Slave Trade, 1440–1870*. New York: Simon and Schuster, 1997.

INTERNET RESOURCES

https://www.npr.org/sections/thesalt/2017/02/10/514385071/frederick-douglass-on-how-slave-owners-used-food-as-a-weapon-of-control

This NPR article discusses the role of food as a means of control over slaves as well as the role of Frederick Douglass in the abolition movement.

https://www.georgiaencyclopedia.org/articles/history-archaeology/slavery-antebellum-georgia

This article shares information about the role of slavery in antebellum Georgia. It contains information about agriculture, statistics about slaveholders, and details about the geography of the South.

https://www.loc.gov/collections/slave-narratives-from-the-federal-writers-project-1936-to-1938/about-this-collection/

Get up close and personal with this collection of slave narratives available through the Library of Congress. Sort through images to read real interviews and recollections of slaves.

https://www.loc.gov/item/ihas.200197495/

African American spirituals played a critical role in the way slaves expressed religion and worshipped. This article delves deeper into the history of these songs and worship practices.

https://docsouth.unc.edu/neh/religiouscontent.html

This resource, provided by the University of North Carolina, provides resources for learning about the religious viewpoints of slaves.

https://www.thirteen.org/wnet/slavery/index.html

Explore this website to learn about different facets of American slavery, including topics related to religion, food, socializing, and family life. It also contains primary documents you can read to explore firsthand accounts of slavery.

http://teachingamericanhistory.org/library/douglass/

Frederick Douglass played an important role in the abolitionist movement. Read more works and speeches by Douglass on this website, which offers quotes and excerpts from his works.

CHRONOLOGY

1641 Massachusetts becomes the first state to officially legalize slavery.

1654 African Americans are legally allowed to own slaves in Virginia. They can now purchase their own family members to free them.

1662 Virginia determines that children would take the slave status of their mothers, and remain slaves for the rest of their lives.

1676 Slaves and indentured servants participate in Bacon's Rebellion. Wealthy white slaveholders became fearful of slave rebellions.

1688 Pennsylvania Quakers pass the first anti-slavery resolution in the future American colonies.

1691 Virginia passes the first anti-miscegenation laws. Marriage between whites and non-whites is now illegal.

1694 South Carolina begins to grow rice, increasing the demand for slaves within the state.

1758 In Philadelphia, Quakers forbid members of the church from owning or trading slaves.

1772 The first slave narrative is written under the name James Albert. More than 100 slave narratives would be written.

1773 The first black church develops in the church. It is located in South Carolina and is called Silver Bluff Baptist Church.

1777 Vermont is the first state to outright ban slavery. All adult males are enfranchised, meaning they are given the right to vote.

1781 Elizabeth Freeman successfully sues her master for her own freedom. Massachusetts ends slavery in the state.

1792 Congress bans African Americans from joining the military. This ban will remain in place until the Civil War.

1804 The first signs of Underground Railroad activity are present, beginning in Pennsylvania.

1807 Congress bans the international slave trade.

1820 The Missouri Compromise admits Maine as a free state and Missouri as a slave state.

1845 *The Narrative of the Life of Frederick Douglass* is published.

1849 Henry "Box" Brown frees himself by having himself mailed to abolitionists in Pennsylvania. That same year, Harriet Tubman escapes from slavery as well.

1852 Harriet Beecher Stowe publishes *Uncle Tom's Cabin*, a book which brought attention to the cruelties of slavery.

1854 The Kansas-Nebraska Act leaves the idea of slavery up to the people who live in the territory.

1857 In *Dred Scott v. Sanford*, the US Supreme Court rules that African Americans cannot have the rights of citizenship.

1860 Abraham Lincoln is elected president of the United States. Southern states declare their intention to secede, and in April 1861 the Civil War begins.

1862 The Militia Act allows President Lincoln to welcome black Americans into the military. It also grants slaves freedom if they join the Union's military.

1863 President Lincoln issues the Emancipation Proclamation, freeing slaves in the rebellious states.

1865 Congress passes and ratifies the Thirteenth Amendment, outlawing slavery.

INDEX

AUTHOR'S BIOGRAPHY

Ashley Nicole is a freelance writer and author with a background in psychology and sociology. Ashley graduated from Northern Arizona University. Though a California native, Ashley now lives in Arizona with her boyfriend and lovely (but noisy) cats.

CREDITS